DATE DUE

What Happens at the ZOO

Cooling off in its pool at the zoo, a polar bear raises a wet paw.

By Judith E. Rinard

BOOKS FOR YOUNG EXPLORERS
NATIONAL GEOGRAPHIC SOCIETY

A mother orangutan cuddles a shy baby named Amanda. They live in a zoo with trees and grassy places. In zoos, animals can care for their babies as they would in the wild.

Binti, a baby chimpanzee, stays close to her parents in their zoo home. The family lives together here, as wild chimpanzees do in Africa. At zoos you can meet animals from all over the world. Let's find out what else happens at the zoo.

What's your favorite animal? Many people love the elephants. At city zoos like this one, you can see many kinds of animals up close.

A zoo police officer shows a boy how to find his favorite animal. Police officers also help keep visitors from hurting the animals or feeding them things that might make them sick.

Some zoos, like this one, are large parks. Standing on a platform, a young visitor looks through a telescope at animals in the distance. He can spot antelopes, hippos, and giraffes by the water. In the open park, the animals run free. Many animals have babies in zoo parks and at other zoos.

A mother giraffe watches over her baby named Sarafu. He is three months old and is already as tall as a man. At the zoo, animals need a lot of care from people, too. It is a busy place.

After checking them for cuts or signs of illness,
a zoo keeper rewards two eager sea lions
with a tasty meal of fish.

In zoo kitchens, workers prepare meals for thousands of animals each day. It's a big job! The workers at sinks are cleaning hundreds of fish for the seals and sea lions.

A diet expert checks food samples. He helps make sure the animals get the foods they need. These dishes hold breakfast for squirrels from Asia. Can you guess what's in their meal?

pen wide! Using a cane as a training tool, a keeper signals an elephant to stay still and lift its trunk. Then the zoo doctor, or veterinarian, looks in the animal's mouth.

Elephants are trained to let keepers and doctors work with them.
A keeper is trimming the toenails of an elephant. If the nails grow too long,
they can crack or become infected. Zoo animals need a lot of special care.

This snow leopard cub named Lama was born at the zoo.
He is six weeks old. A zoo worker called a curator weighs Lama
to see if he is eating enough and growing strong.

Animals can have toothaches or colds just as you can.
A veterinarian checks and cleans a leopard's teeth. She has
given the leopard a drug to make it sleep while she works.
It will wake up soon. Another veterinarian gives a monkey
a checkup. He is listening to its heart and lungs.

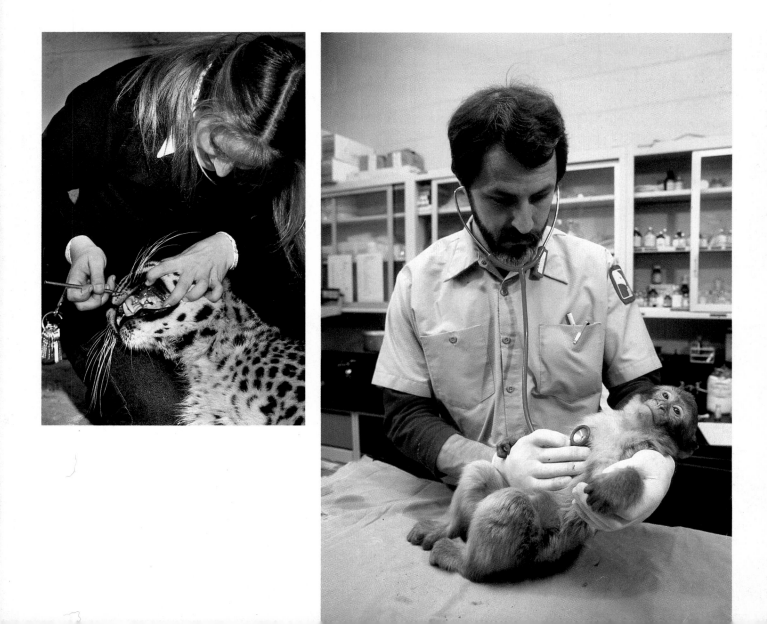

Ling-Ling and her mate are giant pandas. His name is Hsing-Hsing, which is pronounced shing-shing.

Giant pandas like to eat bamboo. They come from China, and there are very few of them left. Zoos are trying to help pandas have young.

Hi! Two young zoo visitors meet a curious white whale. The whale lives in a large tank full of salt water. Through big windows, visitors can watch the whale closely as it swims around. It watches them, too.

Building a new home, or exhibit, for zoo animals takes a lot of work. Artists, builders, and animal experts work together to plan an exhibit. They must decide what things to put in the home to keep the animals healthy and content.

Watching zoo visitors, a female gorilla sits in a tree made of concrete. The ropes and man-made branches give her a chance to climb, swing, and exercise so she will not be bored.

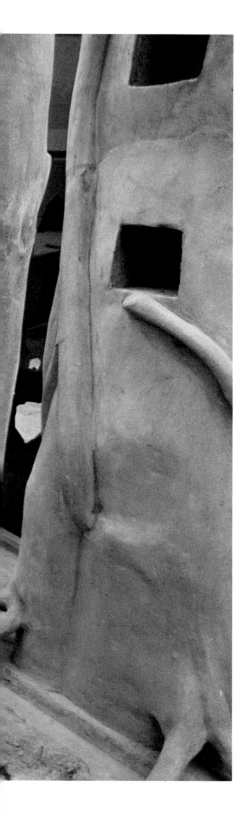

Grrr! A tiger creeps through the grass near a building.
Is this a jungle clearing in Asia? No. It's a zoo home
for Bengal tigers. The big cats sleep inside the building.
The building was made to look like a temple in Asia where
tigers roam free. The open grass gives the tigers space to play.

Visitors can watch the tigers without looking through bars.
A ditch full of water separates the tigers and the people.

At zoos, you can see birds of all colors and sizes. Some live in huge outdoor cages, where they have room to fly, but cannot fly away. They flutter among trees, swim in ponds, and build nests. The indoor home of a mandarin duck looks like a forest floor. Bright yellow parrots greet each other.

A zoo teacher shows some boys and girls a big bird called a turkey vulture. She explains how the bird's strong wings help it glide.

In a special room at this zoo, families learn about animals through games and quizzes. These families study a corn snake, the animal on view that afternoon. The viewing box has a mirror on the bottom, so the snake can be seen from all sides.

Now who's in a box? Two boys pop up next door to a prairie dog. Tunnels under this exhibit allow boys and girls to climb inside a prairie dog town. Children can watch these burrowing animals through viewing holes and learn how it feels to live underground.

My, what big ears! All the better to hear with. Giant "fox ears" teach a girl what it would be like to hear as well as the tiny desert fox does. The fox has extra large ears that help it hear the animals it hunts. Have you ever noticed how sounds seem louder if you hold your hands behind your ears?

In a zoo classroom, another girl pets a little screech owl to feel its soft feathers. These children will also see and touch some animals that have fur and some that have shells. At zoos, you can learn about animals in many different ways.

At the end of the day, a
keeper bathes the elephants.

Zoo animals need care from many people. At night, visitors and most of the workers go home, but guards watch over the animals until morning.

Published by The National Geographic Society
Gilbert M. Grosvenor, *President*
Melvin M. Payne, *Chairman of the Board*
Owen R. Anderson, *Executive Vice President*
Robert L. Breeden, *Vice President, Publications and Educational Media*

Prepared by The Special Publications Division
Donald J. Crump, *Director*
Philip B. Silcott, *Associate Director*
William L. Allen, *Assistant Director*

Staff for this book
Jane H. Buxton, *Managing Editor*
John G. Agnone, *Picture Editor*
Cinda Rose, *Art Director*
Gail N. Hawkins, *Researcher*
Carol Rocheleau Curtis, *Illustrations Assistant*
Nancy F. Berry, Cricket Brazerol, Brenda J. Davis, Mary Elizabeth Davis, Rosamund Garner, Cleo Petroff, Sheryl A. Prohovich,
Nancy E. Simson, Pamela Black Townsend, Virginia A. Williams, *Staff Assistants*

Engraving, Printing, and Product Manufacture
Robert W. Messer, *Manager*
George V. White, *Production Manager*
George J. Zeller, Jr., *Production Project Manager*
Mark R. Dunlevy, David V. Showers, Gregory Storer, *Assistant Production Managers;* Mary A. Bennett, *Production Assistant;*
Julia F. Warner, *Production Staff Assistant*

Consultants
Lynda Ehrlich, *Reading Consultant;* Dr. Glenn O. Blough, *Educational Consultant*
Rodrick Barongi, Curator of Mammals, Metrozoo, Miami, Florida; and Dr. Robert J. Hoage, Special Assistant to the Director,
Michael Morgan, Public Information Specialist, and Judith White, Chief, Office of Education, National Zoological Park,
Smithsonian Institution, Washington, D. C., *Zoo Consultants*

Illustrations Credits
John G. Agnone and Cinda Rose, N.G.S. Staff (cover); E.P.I./Nancy Adams (1); Ira Block (2, 4-5, 12 left); John G. Agnone, N.G.S. Staff (3, 23);
N.G.S. Photographer Joseph H. Bailey (5 right, 8-9, 10 left, 10 right, 11, 15 right, 20-21, 21 right, 26, 30-31); George Elich (6); N.G.S. Photographer
Bates Littlehales (7, 14, 16 left, 25 upper right, 25 lower right, 27, 29); Robert Rattner (12-13); Larry C. Cameron/NIW (15 left, 28); Jessie Cohen,
Office of Graphics and Exhibits, National Zoological Park, Smithsonian Institution (16-17); Annie Griffiths (18-19); Nathan Benn (22); Pat
Vosburgh (24-25, 32).

The Special Publications Division is grateful to the following zoos, which are pictured in this book: Bronx Zoo, New York Zoological Park, Bronx, New
York; Busch Gardens, Tampa, Florida; Cheyenne Mountain Zoological Park, Colorado Springs, Colorado; Fort Worth Zoological Park, Fort Worth,
Texas; Gladys Porter Zoo, Brownsville, Texas; Lion Country Safari, West Palm Beach, Florida; Metrozoo, Miami, Florida; Minnesota Zoological
Garden, Apple Valley, Minnesota; National Zoological Park, Smithsonian Institution, Washington, D. C.; Riverbanks Zoological Park, Columbia,
South Carolina; San Diego Wild Animal Park, Escondido, California; San Diego Zoological Park, San Diego, California.

Safe in its zoo home,
a sleepy kit fox naps
in the sunshine.
COVER: A zoo keeper feeds
milk to a baby monkey
whose mother was not able
to care for it. When the
monkey grows stronger,
it will live with other
monkeys at the zoo.

Library of Congress CIP Data
Rinard, Judith E., 1947-
    What happens at the zoo.
    (Books for young explorers)
    Summary: Describes the functions of a zoo and the care and
treatment given to the animals that live there.
    1. Zoos – Juvenile literature.   2. Zoo animals – Juvenile literature.
[1. Zoos. 2. Zoo animals]
    I. Title. II. Series.
QL76.R558 1984   590'.74'4   84-14876
ISBN 0-87044-524-3 (regular edition)
ISBN 0-87044-529-4 (library edition)